The Key Facts™ on

Peru

Essential Information on Peru

By Patrick W. Nee

The Internationalist®

www.internationalist.com

The Internationalist®

International Business, Investment, and Travel

Published by:

The Internationalist Publishing Company

96 Walter Street/ Suite 200

Boston, MA 02131, USA

Tel: 617-354-7722

www.internationalist.com

PN@internationalist.com

The Internationalist is a Registered Trademark. "Key Facts" and "The Internationalist Business Guides" are Trademarks of The Internationalist Publishing Company.

All Rights are reserved under International, Pan-American, and Pan-Asian Conventions. No part of this book may be reproduced in any form without the written permission of the publisher. All rights vigorously enforced

Table Of Contents

Chapter 1: Background

Chapter 2: Geography

Chapter 3: People and Society

Chapter 4: Government and Key Leaders

Chapter 5: Economy

Chapter 6: Energy

Chapter 7: Communications

Chapter 8: Transportation

Chapter 9: Military

Chapter 10: Transnational Issues

Map of Peru

Chapter 1: Background

Ancient Peru was the seat of several prominent Andean civilizations, most notably that of the Incas whose empire was captured by Spanish conquistadors in 1533. Peruvian independence was declared in 1821, and remaining Spanish forces were defeated in 1824. After a dozen years of military rule, Peru returned to democratic leadership in 1980, but experienced economic problems and the growth of a violent insurgency. President Alberto FUJIMORI's election in 1990 ushered in a decade that saw a dramatic turnaround in the economy and significant progress in curtailing guerrilla activity. Nevertheless, the president's increasing reliance on authoritarian measures and an economic slump in the late 1990s generated mounting dissatisfaction with his regime, which led to his ouster in 2000. A caretaker government oversaw new elections in the spring of 2001, which installed Alejandro TOLEDO Manrique as the new head of government - Peru's first democratically elected president of indigenous Quechuan ethnicity. The presidential election of 2006 saw the return of Alan GARCIA Perez who, after a disappointing presidential term from 1985 to 1990, oversaw a robust economic rebound. In June 2011, former army officer Ollanta HUMALA Tasso was elected president, defeating Keiko FUJIMORI Higuchi, the daughter of Alberto FUJIMORI. Since his election, HUMALA has carried on the sound, market-oriented economic policies of the three preceding administrations.

Chapter 2: Geography

Location:
> Western South America, bordering the South Pacific Ocean, between Chile and Ecuador

Geographic coordinates:
10 00 S, 76 00 W

Map references:
> South America

Area:
> total: 1,285,216 sq km
> country comparison to the world: 20
> land: 1,279,996 sq km
> water: 5,220 sq km

Area - comparative:
> slightly smaller than Alaska

Land boundaries:
> total: 7,461 km
> border countries: Bolivia 1,075 km, Brazil 2,995 km, Chile 171 km, Colombia 1,800 km, Ecuador 1,420 km

Coastline:
2,414 km

Maritime claims:
>territorial sea: 200 nm
>
>continental shelf: 200 nm

Climate:
>varies from tropical in east to dry desert in west; temperate to frigid in Andes

Terrain:
>western coastal plain (costa), high and rugged Andes in center (sierra), eastern lowland jungle of Amazon Basin (selva)

Elevation extremes:
>lowest point: Pacific Ocean 0 m
>
>highest point: Nevado Huascaran 6,768 m

Natural resources:
>copper, silver, gold, petroleum, timber, fish, iron ore, coal, phosphate, potash, hydropower, natural gas

Land use:
>arable land: 2.84%
>
>permanent crops: 0.66%
>
>other: 96.5% (2011)

Irrigated land:
>11,960 sq km (2003)

Total renewable water resources:
1,913 cu km (2011)

Freshwater withdrawal (domestic/industrial/agricultural):
total: 19.34 cu km/yr (8%/10%/82%)
per capita: 727.6 cu m/yr (2005)

Natural hazards:
earthquakes, tsunamis, flooding, landslides, mild volcanic activity
volcanism: volcanic activity in the Andes Mountains; Ubinas (elev. 5,672 m), which last erupted in 2009, is the country's most active volcano; other historically active volcanoes include El Misti, Huaynaputina, Sabancaya, and Yucamane

Environment - current issues:
deforestation (some the result of illegal logging); overgrazing of the slopes of the costa and sierra leading to soil erosion; desertification; air pollution in Lima; pollution of rivers and coastal waters from municipal and mining wastes

Environment - international agreements:
party to: Antarctic-Environmental Protocol, Antarctic-Marine Living Resources, Antarctic Treaty, Biodiversity, Climate Change, Climate Change-Kyoto Protocol, Desertification,

Endangered Species, Hazardous Wastes, Marine Dumping, Ozone Layer Protection, Ship Pollution, Tropical Timber 83, Tropical Timber 94, Wetlands, Whaling
<u>signed, but not ratified:</u> none of the selected agreements

Geography - note:
shares control of Lago Titicaca, world's highest navigable lake, with Bolivia; a remote slope of Nevado Mismi, a 5,316 m peak, is the ultimate source of the Amazon River

Chapter 3: People and Society

Nationality:

noun: Peruvian(s)

adjective: Peruvian

Ethnic groups:

Amerindian 45%, mestizo (mixed Amerindian and white) 37%, white 15%, black, Japanese, Chinese, and other 3%

Languages:

Spanish (official) 84.1%, Quechua (official) 13%, Aymara (official) 1.7%, Ashaninka 0.3%, other native languages (includes a large number of minor Amazonian languages) 0.7%, other 0.2% (2007 Census)

Religions:

Roman Catholic 81.3%, Evangelical 12.5%, other 3.3%, unspecified or none 2.9% (2007 Census)

Population:

29,849,303 (July 2013 est.)

country comparison to the world: 43

Age structure:

0-14 years: 27.6% (male 4,197,698/female 4,053,852)

15-24 years: 19.4% (male 2,894,420/female 2,891,714)

25-54 years: 39.2% (male 5,633,249/female 6,056,017)

55-64 years: 7.1% (male 1,039,975/female 1,086,428)

65 years and over: 6.7% (male 947,349/female 1,048,601) (2013 est.)

Median age:

total: 26.7 years

male: 26 years

female: 27.4 years (2013 est.)

Population growth rate:

1% (2013 est.)

country comparison to the world: 115

Birth rate:

18.85 births/1,000 population (2013 est.)

country comparison to the world: 98

Death rate:

5.97 deaths/1,000 population (2013 est.)

country comparison to the world: 165

Net migration rate:
-2.86 migrant(s)/1,000 population (2013 est.)
country comparison to the world: 174

Urbanization:
urban population: 77% of total population (2010)
rate of urbanization: 1.6% annual rate of change (2010-15 est.)

Major urban areas - population:
LIMA (capital) 8.769 million; Arequipa 778,000 (2009)

Sex ratio:
at birth: 1.05 male(s)/female
0-14 years: 1.04 male(s)/female
15-24 years: 1 male(s)/female
25-54 years: 0.93 male(s)/female
55-64 years: 0.96 male(s)/female
65 years and over: 0.9 male(s)/female
total population: 0.97 male(s)/female (2013 est.)

Maternal mortality rate:
67 deaths/100,000 live births (2010)
country comparison to the world: 91

Infant mortality rate:
total: 20.85 deaths/1,000 live births
country comparison to the world: 89
male: 23.1 deaths/1,000 live births
female: 18.49 deaths/1,000 live births (2013 est.)

Life expectancy at birth:
total population: 72.98 years
country comparison to the world: 128
male: 71.01 years
female: 75.05 years (2013 est.)

Total fertility rate:
2.25 children born/woman (2013 est.)
country comparison to the world: 98

Health expenditures:
4.8% of GDP (2011)
country comparison to the world: 145

Physicians density:
0.92 physicians/1,000 population (2009)

Hospital bed density:
1.5 beds/1,000 population (2011)

Drinking water source:
improved:
urban: 90.9% of population
rural: 66.1% of population
total: 85.3% of population
unimproved:
urban: 9.1% of population
rural: 33.9% of population
total: 14.7% of population (2011 est.)

Sanitation facility access:
improved:
urban: 81.3% of population
rural: 38.4% of population
total: 71.6% of population
unimproved:
urban: 18.7% of population
rural: 61.6% of population
total: 28.4% of population (2011 est.)

HIV/AIDS - adult prevalence rate:
0.4% (2009 est.)
country comparison to the world: 73

HIV/AIDS - people living with HIV/AIDS:
75,000 (2009 est.)
country comparison to the world: 48

HIV/AIDS - deaths:
5,000 (2009 est.)
country comparison to the world: 38
Major infectious diseases:
degree of risk: very high
food or waterborne diseases: bacterial diarrhea, hepatitis A, and typhoid fever
vectorborne diseases: dengue fever, malaria, and Bartonellosis (Oroya fever) (2013)
Obesity - adult prevalence rate:
15.7% (2008)
country comparison to the world: 117
Education expenditures:
2.6% of GDP (2011)
country comparison to the world: 155
Literacy:
definition: age 15 and over can read and write
total population: 89.6%
male: 94.9%
female: 84.6% (2007 est.)
School life expectancy (primary to tertiary education):
total: 13 years
male: 13 years
female: 13 years (2010)

Unemployment, youth ages 15-24:
    total: 16.2% (2011)
    country comparison to the world: 81

Chapter 4: Government and Key Leaders

Country name:

    conventional long form: Republic of Peru

    conventional short form: Peru

    local long form: Republica del Peru

    local short form: Peru

Government type:

    constitutional republic

Capital:

    name: Lima

    geographic coordinates: 12 03 S, 77 03 W

    time difference: UTC-5 (same time as Washington, DC during Standard Time)

Administrative divisions:

    25 regions (regiones, singular - region) and 1 province* (provincia); Amazonas, Ancash, Apurimac, Arequipa, Ayacucho, Cajamarca, Callao, Cusco, Huancavelica, Huanuco, Ica, Junin, La Libertad, Lambayeque, Lima, Lima*, Loreto, Madre de Dios, Moquegua, Pasco, Piura, Puno, San Martin, Tacna, Tumbes, Ucayali

Independence:
28 July 1821 (from Spain)

National holiday:
Independence Day, 28 July (1821)

Constitution:
several previous; latest promulgated 29 December 1993, enacted 31 December 1993; amended several times, last in 2009 (2009)

Legal system:
civil law system

International law organization participation:
accepts compulsory ICJ jurisdiction with reservations; accepts ICCt jurisdiction

Suffrage:
18 years of age; universal and compulsory until the age of 70

Executive branch:
chief of state: President Ollanta HUMALA Tasso (since 28 July 2011); First Vice President Marisol ESPINOZA Cruz (since 28 July 2011); Second Vice President (vacant); note - the president is both the chief of state and head of government

head of government: President Ollanta HUMALA Tasso (since 28 July 2011); First Vice President Marisol ESPINOZA Cruz (since 28 July 2011); Second Vice President (vacant)
cabinet: Council of Ministers appointed by the president
elections: president elected by popular vote for a five-year term (eligible for nonconsecutive reelection); presidential and congressional elections last held on 10 April 2011 with runoff election held on 6 June 2011 (next to be held in April 2016)
election results: Ollanta HUMALA Tasso elected president in runoff election; percent of vote - Ollanta HUMALA Tasso 51.5%, Keiko FUJIMORI Higuchi 48.5%

Legislative branch:

unicameral Congress of the Republic of Peru or Congreso de la Republica del Peru (130 seats; members are elected by popular vote to serve five-year terms)
elections: last held on 10 April 2011 (next to be held in April 2016)

election results: percent of vote by party - Gana Peru 25.3%, Fuerza 2011 23%, PP 14.8%, Alliance for Great Change 14.4%, National Solidarity 10.2%, Peruvian Aprista Party 6.4%, other 5.9%; seats by party - Gana Peru 47, Fuerza 2011 37, PP 21, Alliance for Great Change 12, National Solidarity 9, Peruvian Aprista Party 4; note - defections by members of National Assembly are commonplace, resulting in frequent changes in the numbers of seats held by the various parties

Judicial branch:

Highest court(s): Supreme Court (consists of 16 judges and divided into civil, criminal, and constitutional-social sectors)

Judge selection and term of offfice: justices proposed by the National Council of the Judiciary or National Judicial Council (a 7-member independent body), nominated by the president, and confirmed by the Congress (all appointments reviewed by the Council every 7 years; justices appointed for life or until age 70 subordinate courts: Court of Constitutional Guarantees; Superior Courts or Cortes Superiores; specialized civil, criminal, and mixed courts; two types of peace courts in which professional judges and selected members of the local communities preside

Political parties and leaders:
Alliance for Great Change (Alianza por el Gran Cambio) (a coalition of the Alliance for Progress, Humanist Party, National Restoration Party, and Popular Christian Party) [Pedro Pablo KUCZYNSKI]
Fuerza 2011 [Keiko FUJIMORI Higuchi]
Gana Peru (a coalition of Lima Para Todos, Peruvian Communist Party, Peruvian Nationalist Party, and Peruvian Socialist Party) [Ollanta HUMALA Tasso]
National Solidarity (Solidaridad Nacional) or SN (a coalition of Cambio 90, Siempre Unidos, Todos por el Peru, and Union for Peru or UPP) [Luis CASTANEDA Lossio]
Peru Posible or PP (a coalition of Accion Popular and Somos Peru) [Alejandro TOLEDO Manrique]
Peruvian Aprista Party (Partido Aprista Peruano) or PAP [Alan GARCIA Perez] (also referred to by its original name Alianza Popular Revolucionaria Americana or APRA)

Political pressure groups and leaders:
General Workers Confederation of Peru (Confederacion General de Trabajadores del Peru) or CGTP [Mario HUAMAN]

Shining Path (Sendero Luminoso) or SL [Abimael GUZMAN Reynoso (imprisoned), Victor QUISPE Palomino (top leader at-large)] (leftist guerrilla group)

International organization participation:
APEC, BIS, CAN, CD, CELAC, EITI (compliant country), FAO, G-24, G-77, IADB, IAEA, IBRD, ICAO, ICC (NGOs), ICRM, IDA, IFAD, IFC, IFRCS, IHO, ILO, IMF, IMO, IMSO, Interpol, IOC, IOM, IPU, ISO, ITSO, ITU, ITUC (NGOs), LAES, LAIA, Mercosur (associate), MIGA, MINURSO, MINUSTAH, MONUSCO, NAM, OAS, OPANAL, OPCW, PCA, SICA (observer), UN, UNASUR, UNCTAD, UNESCO, UNIDO, Union Latina, UNISFA, UNMIL, UNMISS, UNOCI, UNWTO, UPU, WCO, WFTU (NGOs), WHO, WIPO, WMO, WTO

Diplomatic representation in the US:
chief of mission: Ambassador Harold Winston FORSYTH Mejia (since 29 August 2011)
chancery: 1700 Massachusetts Avenue NW, Washington, DC 20036
telephone: [1] (202) 833-9860 through 9869

FAX: [1] (202) 659-8124

Consulate(s) general: Atlanta, Boston, Chicago, Dallas, Denver, Hartford (CT), Houston, Los Angeles, Miami, New York, Paterson (NJ), San Francisco

Diplomatic representation from the US:

chief of mission: Ambassador (vacant); Charge d'Affaires Michael J. Fitzpatrick (since 20 September 2013)

embassy: Avenida La Encalada, Cuadra 17 s/n, Surco, Lima 33

mailing address: P. O. Box 1995, Lima 1; American Embassy (Lima), APO AA 34031-5000

telephone: [51] (1) 618-2000

FAX: [51] (1) 618-2397

Key Leaders:
Pres.
 Ollanta Moises HUMALA Tasso
First Vice Pres.
 Marisol ESPINOZA Cruz
Prime Min.
 Juan Federico JIMENEZ Mayor

Min. of Agriculture
Milton VON HESSE La Serna
Min. of Culture
Diana ALVAREZ Calderon Gallo
Min. of Defense
Pedro CATERIANO Bellido
Min. of Economy & Finance
Luis Miguel CASTILLA Rubio
Min. of Education
Patricia SALAS O'Brien
Min. of Energy & Mines
Jorge HUMBERTO Merino Tafur
Min. of Environment
Manuel Gerardo Pedro PULGAR-VIDAL
Min. of Foreign Relations
Eda Adriana RIVAS Franchini
Min. of Foreign Trade & Tourism
Blanca Magali SILVA Velarde-Alvarez
Min. of Health
Midori Musme DE HABICH Rospigliosi
Min. of Housing
Rene CORNEJO Diaz
Min. of Interior
Wilfredo PEDRAZA Sierra

Min. of Justice
Daniel Augusto FIGALLO Rivadeneyra
Min. of Labor
Teresa LAOS
Min. of Production
Gladys TRIVENO Chan Jan
Min. of Social Inclusion & Development
Monica RUBIO Garcia
Min. of Transportation & Communications
Carlos PAREDES Rodriguez
Min. of Women & Social Development
Ana JARA Velasquez
Pres., Central Reserve Bank
Julio VELARDE
Ambassador to the US
Harold Winston FORSYTH Mejia
Permanent Representative to the UN, New York
Gustavo Adolf Mez-Cuadra VELASQUEZ

Flag description:
three equal, vertical bands of red (hoist side), white, and red with the coat of arms centered in the white band; the coat of arms features a shield bearing a vicuna (representing fauna), a

cinchona tree (the source of quinine, signifying flora), and a yellow cornucopia spilling out coins (denoting mineral wealth); red recalls blood shed for independence, white symbolizes peace

National symbol(s):

vicuna (a camelid related to the llama)

National anthem:

name: "Himno Nacional del Peru" (National Anthem of Peru)

Chapter 5: Economy

Economy - overview:
Peru's economy reflects its varied geography - an arid lowland coastal region, the central high sierra of the Andes, the dense forest of the Amazon, with tropical lands bordering Colombia and Brazil. A wide range of important mineral resources are found in the mountainous and coastal areas, and Peru's coastal waters provide excellent fishing grounds. The Peruvian economy has been growing by an average of 6.4% per year since 2002 with a stable/slightly appreciating exchange rate and low inflation, which in 2013 is expected to be below the upper limit of the Central Bank target range of 1 to 3%. Growth has been in the 6-9% range for the last three years, due partly to a leap in private investment, especially in the extractive sector, which accounts for more than 60% of Peru's total exports. Despite Peru's strong macroeconomic performance, dependence on minerals and metals exports and imported foodstuffs subjects the economy to fluctuations in world prices. Poor infrastructure hinders the spread of growth to Peru's non-coastal areas. Peru's rapid expansion

coupled with cash transfers and other programs have helped to reduce the national poverty rate by 23 percentage points since 2002, but inequality persists and continues to pose a challenge for the new Ollanta HUMALA administration, which has championed a policy of social inclusion and a more equitable distribution of income. Peru's free trade policy has continued under the HUMALA administration; since 2006, Peru has signed trade deals with the US, Canada, Singapore, China, Korea, Mexico, Japan, the European Free Trade Association, Chile, and four other countries; concluded negotiations with Venezuela, Costa Rica, and Guatemala; and begun trade talks with two other Central American countries and the Trans-Pacific Partnership. Peru also has signed a trade pact with Chile, Colombia, and Mexico called the Pacific Alliance that rivals Mercosur in combined population, GDP, and trade. The US-Peru Trade Promotion Agreement entered into force 1 February 2009, opening the way to greater trade and investment between the two economies. Although Peru has continued to attract foreign investment, political activism and protests are hampering development of some projects related to natural resource extraction.

GDP (purchasing power parity):
$322.9 billion (2012 est.)
country comparison to the world: 42
$303.8 billion (2011 est.)
$284.3 billion (2010 est.)
note: data are in 2012 US dollars

GDP (official exchange rate):
$196.2 billion (2012 est.)

GDP - real growth rate:
6.3% (2012 est.)
country comparison to the world: 38
6.9% (2011 est.)
8.8% (2010 est.)

GDP - per capita (PPP):
$10,600 (2012 est.)
country comparison to the world: 112
$10,100 (2011 est.)
$9,600 (2010 est.)
note: data are in 2012 US dollars

GDP - composition by sector:
    agriculture: 6.3%
    industry: 37.6%
    services: 56.1% (2012 est.)

Labor force:
    11.02 million
    country comparison to the world: 50

Labor force - by occupation:
    agriculture: 0.7%
    industry: 23.8%
    services: 75.5% (2005)

Unemployment rate:
    5.2% (2012 est.)
    country comparison to the world: 48
    7.9% (2011 est.)

Population below poverty line:
    27.8% (2011 est.)

Household income or consumption by percentage share:
    lowest 10%: 1.4%
    highest 10%: 36.1% (2010 est.)

Distribution of family income - Gini index:
    46 (2010)
    country comparison to the world: 34
    51 (2005)

Budget:
    revenues: $62.19 billion
    expenditures: $57.9 billion (2012 est.)

Taxes and other revenues:
    31.7% of GDP (2012 est.)
    country comparison to the world: 87

Budget surplus (+) or deficit (-):
    2.2% of GDP (2012 est.)
    country comparison to the world: 20

Public debt:
    16.6% of GDP (2012 est.)
    country comparison to the world: 136
    19.9% of GDP (2011 est.)

Inflation rate (consumer prices):
    3.7% (2012 est.)
    country comparison to the world: 115
    3.4% (2011 est.)

Fiscal year:
    Calendar year

Central bank discount rate:
    5.05% (31 December 2012)
    country comparison to the world: 68
    5.05% (31 December 2011)

Commercial bank prime lending rate:

19.23% (31 December 2012 est.)

country comparison to the world: 22

18.69% (31 December 2011 est.)

Stock of narrow money:

$32.61 billion (31 December 2012 est.)

country comparison to the world: 58

$25.15 billion (31 December 2011 est.)

Stock of broad money:

$73.97 billion (31 December 2012 est.)

country comparison to the world: 60

$64.6 billion (31 December 2011 est.)

Stock of domestic credit:

$36.76 billion (31 December 2012 est.)

country comparison to the world: 66

$33.15 billion (31 December 2011 est.)

Market value of publicly traded shares:

$153.4 billion (31 December 2012)

country comparison to the world: 38

$$121.6 billion (31 December 2011)

$160.9 billion (31 December 2010)

Current account balance:
$-7.137 billion (2012 est.)
country comparison to the world: 170
$-3.341 billion (2011 est.)

Exports:
$45.64 billion (2012 est.)
country comparison to the world: 61
$46.27 billion (2011 est.)

Exports - commodities:
copper, gold, lead, zinc, tin, iron ore, molybdenum, silver; crude petroleum and petroleum products, natural gas; coffee, asparagus and other vegetables, fruit, apparel and textiles, fishmeal, fish, chemicals, fabricated metal products and machinery, alloys

Exports - partners:
China 19.9%, US 15.7%, Canada 9.5%, Japan 6.6%, Spain 5.2%, Chile 4.9% (2012)

Imports:
$41.11 billion (2012 est.)
country comparison to the world: 59
$36.97 billion (2011 est.)

Imports - commodities:
petroleum and petroleum products, chemicals, plastics, machinery, vehicles, color TV sets, power shovels, front-end loaders, telephones and telecommunication equipment, iron and steel, wheat, corn, soybean products, paper, cotton, vaccines and medicines

Imports - partners:
US 24.6%, China 14%, Brazil 6.4%, Argentina 5%, Chile 4.8%, Colombia 4.2%, Ecuador 4.1%, Mexico 4% (2012)

Reserves of foreign exchange and gold:
$64.17 billion (31 December 2012 est.)
country comparison to the world: 32
$48.93 billion (31 December 2011 est.)

Debt - external:
$50.47 billion (31 December 2012 est.)
country comparison to the world: 62
$44.87 billion (31 December 2011 est.)

Stock of direct foreign investment - at home:
$63.51 billion (31 December 2012 est.)
country comparison to the world: 49
$51.21 billion (31 December 2011 est.)

Stock of direct foreign investment - abroad:

$3.041 billion (31 December 2012 est.)

country comparison to the world: 69

$3.099 billion (31 December 2011 est.)

Exchange rates:

nuevo sol (PEN) per US dollar -
2.6376 (2012 est.)
2.7541 (2011 est.)
2.8251 (2010 est.)
3.0115 (2009)
2.91 (2008)

Chapter 6: Energy

Electricity - production:
38.4 billion kWh (2012 est.)
country comparison to the world: 60

Electricity - consumption:
34.25 billion kWh (2011 est.)
country comparison to the world: 59

Electricity - exports:
112 million kWh (2010 est.)
country comparison to the world: 74

Electricity - imports:
0 kWh (2012 est.)
country comparison to the world: 119

Electricity - installed generating capacity:
8.613 million kW (2010 est.)
country comparison to the world: 61

Electricity - from fossil fuels:
60.1% of total installed capacity (2010 est.)
country comparison to the world: 134

Electricity - from nuclear fuels:
0% of total installed capacity (2010 est.)
country comparison to the world: 159

Electricity - from hydroelectric plants:

39.9% of total installed capacity (2010 est.)

country comparison to the world: 60

Electricity - from other renewable sources:

0% of total installed capacity (2010 est.)

country comparison to the world: 110

Crude oil - production:

160,400 bbl/day (2012 est.)

country comparison to the world: 42

Crude oil - exports:

15,610 bbl/day (2012 est.)

country comparison to the world: 55

Crude oil - imports:

99,590 bbl/day (2012 est.)

country comparison to the world: 50

Crude oil - proved reserves:

579.2 million bbl (1 January 2013 es)

country comparison to the world: 49

Refined petroleum products - production:

159,500 bbl/day (2012 est.)

country comparison to the world: 62

Refined petroleum products - consumption:

206,900 bbl/day (2012 est.)

country comparison to the world: 56

Refined petroleum products - exports:

82,080 bbl/day (2012 est.)

country comparison to the world: 49

Refined petroleum products - imports:

43,480 bbl/day (2012 est.)

country comparison to the world: 76

Natural gas - production:

32.4 billion cu m (2012)

country comparison to the world: 28

Natural gas - consumption:

5.49 billion cu m (2010 est.)

country comparison to the world: 58

Natural gas - exports:

8.73 billion cu m (2012 est.)

country comparison to the world: 30

Natural gas - imports:

0 cu m (2012)

country comparison to the world: 115

Natural gas - proved reserves:

6359.6 billion cu m (1 January 2013 es)

country comparison to the world: 38

Carbon dioxide emissions from consumption of energy:

37.71 million Mt (2011 est.)

country comparison to the world: 70

Chapter 7: Communications

Telephones - main lines in use:
    3.42 million (2012)
    country comparison to the world: 45

Telephones - mobile cellular:
    29.4 million (2012)
    country comparison to the world: 36

Telephone system:
    general assessment: adequate for most requirements; nationwide microwave radio relay system and a domestic satellite system with 12 earth stations
    domestic: fixed-line teledensity is only about 12 per 100 persons; mobile-cellular teledensity, spurred by competition among multiple providers, exceeds 100 telephones per 100 persons
    international: country code - 51; the South America-1 (SAM-1) and Pan American (PAN-AM) submarine cable systems provide links to parts of Central and South America, the Caribbean, and US; satellite earth stations - 2 Intelsat (Atlantic Ocean) (2010)

Broadcast media:
10 major TV networks of which only one, Television Nacional de Peru, is state-owned; multi-channel cable TV services are available; in excess of 2,000 radio stations including a substantial number of indigenous language stations (2010)

Internet country code:
.pe

Internet hosts:
234,102 (2012)
country comparison to the world: 70

Internet users:
9.158 million (2009)
country comparison to the world: 31

Chapter 8: Transportation

Airports:
    191 (2013)
    country comparison to the world: 30

Airports - with paved runways:
    total: 59
    over 3,047 m: 5
    2,438 to 3,047 m: 21
    1,524 to 2,437 m: 16
    914 to 1,523 m: 12
    under 914 m: 5 (2013)

Airports - with unpaved runways:
    total: 132
    over 3,047 m: 5
    2,438 to 3,047 m: 21
    1,524 to 2,437: 16
    914 to 1,523 m: 12
    under 914 m: 5 (2013)

Heliports:
    5 (2013)

Pipelines:
>extra heavy crude 786 km; gas 1,526 km; liquid petroleum gas 679 km; oil 1,033 km; refined products 15 km (2013)

Railways:
>total: 1,907 km
>
>country comparison to the world: 74
>
>standard gauge: 1,722 km 1.435-m gauge
>
>narrow gague: 135 km 0.914-m gauge (2012)

Roadways:
>total: 140,672 km (of which 18,698 km are paved)
>
>country comparison to the world: 35

Waterways:
>8,808 km (there are 8,600 km of navigable tributaries on the Amazon system and 208 km on Lago Titicaca) (2011)
>
>country comparison to the world: 14

Merchant marine:
>total: 22
>
>country comparison to the world: 92
>
>by type: cargo 2, chemical tanker 5, liquefied gas 2, petroleum tanker 13
>
>registered in other countries: 9 (Panama 9) (2010)

Ports and terminals:
>Major seaports: Callao, Matarani, Paita
>River ports: Iquitos, Pucallpa, Yurimaguas (Amazon)
>Oil terminals: Conchan oil terminal, La Pampilla oil terminal
>Container ports (TEUs): Callao (1,616,365)

Chapter 9: Military

Military branches:
>Peruvian Army (Ejercito Peruano), Peruvian Navy (Marina de Guerra del Peru, MGP; includes naval air, naval infantry, and Coast Guard), Air Force of Peru (Fuerza Aerea del Peru, FAP) (2013)

Military service age and obligation:
>18-50 years of age for male and 18-45 years of age for female voluntary military service; no conscription (2012)

Manpower available for military service:
>males age 16-49: 7,385,588
>females age 16-49: 37,727,623 (2010 est.)

Manpower fit for military service:
>males age 16-49: 5,788,629
>females age 16-49: 6,565,097 (2010 est.)

Manpower reaching militarily significant age annually:
>male: 304,094
>female: 298,447 (2010 est.)

Military expenditures:
>1.28% of GDP (2012)
>country comparison to the world: 246

Chapter 10: Transnational Issues

Disputes - international:
Chile and Ecuador rejected Peru's November 2005 unilateral legislation to shift the axis of their joint treaty-defined maritime boundaries along the parallels of latitude to equidistance lines which favor Peru; organized illegal narcotics operations in Colombia have penetrated Peru's shared border; Peru rejects Bolivia's claim to restore maritime access through a sovereign corridor through Chile along the Peruvian border

Refugees and internally displaced persons:
IDPs: 150,000 (civil war from 1980-2000; most IDPs are indigenous peasants in Andean and Amazonian regions; as of 2011, no new information on the situation of these IDPs) (2011)

Illicit drugs:
until 1996 the world's largest coca leaf producer, Peru is now the world's second largest producer of coca leaf, though it lags far behind Colombia; cultivation of coca in Peru was estimated at 40,000 hectares in 2009, a slight decrease over 2008; second largest producer of cocaine, estimated at 225 metric tons of potential pure cocaine in 2009; finished cocaine is shipped out from Pacific ports to the international drug market; increasing amounts of base and finished cocaine, however, are being moved to Brazil, Chile, Argentina, and Bolivia for use in the Southern Cone or transshipment to Europe and Africa; increasing domestic drug consumption

Map of Peru

Other Key Facts™ Titles

Key Facts on Syria

Key Facts on China

Key Facts on Qatar

Key Facts on India

Key Facts on Germany

Key Facts on Argentina

Key Facts on Russia

Key Facts on North Korea

Key Facts on Brazil

Key Facts on Italy

Key Facts on the United Arab Emirates

Key Facts on the European Union

Key Facts on Pakistan

Key Facts on Saudi Arabia

Key Facts on Cyprus

Key Facts on Iran

Key Facts on Afghanistan

Key Facts on Iraq

Key Facts on Indonesia

Key Facts on South Korea

Key Facts on France

Key Facts on the United Kingdom

Key Facts on Egypt

Key Facts on Israel

All Key Facts™ Titles are Available at

www.Amazon.com

THE INTERNATIONALIST®

2014

WWW.INTERNATIONALIST.COM

www.ingramcontent.com/pod-product-compliance
Lightning Source LLC
Chambersburg PA
CBHW071823170526
45167CB00003B/1401